Fact Finders™

Questions and Answers: Countries

Ethiopia

A Question and Answer Book

by Mary Englar

Consultant:
David Sandgren
Professor of History
Concordia College
Moorhead, Minnesota

Capstone press

Mankato, Minnesota

Fact Finders is published by Capstone Press,
151 Good Counsel Drive, P.O. Box 669, Mankato, Minnesota 56002.
www.capstonepress.com

Library of Congress Cataloging-in-Publication Data
Englar, Mary.
    Ethiopia : a question and answer book / by Mary Englar.
    p. cm.—(Fact finders. Questions and answers. Countries)
Summary: "Describes the geography, history, economy, and culture of Ethiopia in a
    question-and-answer format"–Provided by publisher.
    ISBN 0–7368–4354–X
    1. Ethiopia—Miscellanea—Juvenile literature. I. Title. II. Series.
DT374.E54 2006
963—dc22   2005001167

Editorial Credits
Silver Editions, editorial, design, and production; Kia Adams, set designer; Ortelius Design,
Inc., cartographer; Wanda Winch, photo researcher; Scott Thoms, photo editor

Photo Credits
Art Directors/A. Gasson, 4; Brian Seed, 6–7; Jane Sweeney, cover (background), 13
Corbis/Earl & Nazima Kowall, 17; Jim Sugar, 25; Jon Hicks, 10–11
Getty Images Inc./Ian Waldie, 19
Jason Laurè, 12, 24
Larry Luxner, 14–15
One Mile Up, Inc. 29 (flag)
Peter Arnold, Inc./Patricia Jordan, cover (foreground)
Photo Courtesy of Paul Baker, 29 (coins)
Photo Courtesy of Richard Sutherland, 29 (bill)
Victor Englebert, 1, 9, 21, 22–23, 27

1 2 3 4 5 6 10 09 08 07 06 05

Table of Contents

Features

Where is Ethiopia?

Ethiopia is in eastern Africa. It is almost two times bigger than the U.S. state of Texas.

Mountains and **highlands** cover much of Ethiopia. The Great Rift Valley divides the highlands into two areas. In the northwest, uneven valleys cut between the mountains. The Blue Nile River begins at Lake Tana. It winds through the western mountains.

The Blue Nile Falls are also known as the Smoke and Fire Falls.

4

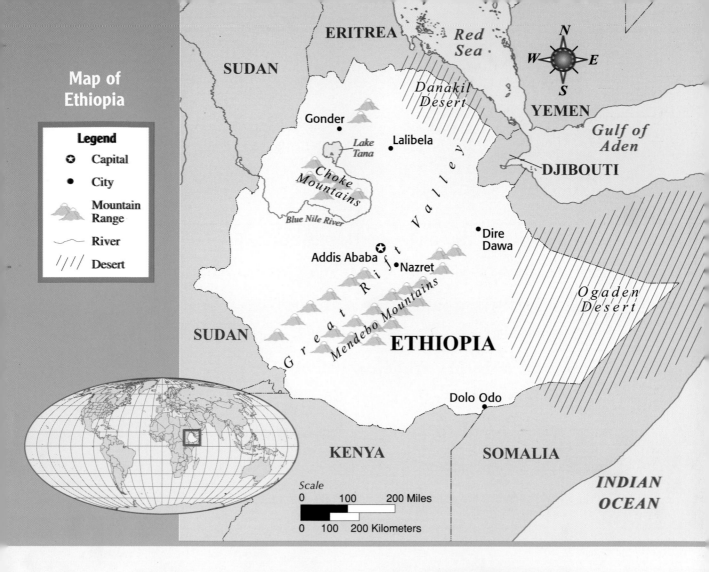

Legend

⊙   Capital

•   City

   Mountain
   Range

‿   River

////   Desert

ERITREA

SUDAN

Red
Sea

Danakil
Desert

YEMEN

Gulf of
Aden

DJIBOUTI

Gonder

Lake
Tana

Lalibela

Choke
Mountains

Blue Nile River

Great Rift Valley

Dire
Dawa

Addis Ababa

Nazret

Mendebo Mountains

ETHIOPIA

Ogaden
Desert

SUDAN

Dolo Odo

KENYA

SOMALIA

INDIAN
OCEAN

Scale

0   100   200 Miles

0   100   200 Kilometers

In the southeast, the highlands slope
toward desert lowlands. The east receives
little rain. Many places receive less than
8 inches (20 centimeters) each year. The
mountains and central highlands usually
get plenty of rain. Some places receive about
40 inches (102 centimeters) each year.

When did Ethiopia become a country?

Ethiopia is the oldest independent country in Africa. About 2,000 years ago, the Aksum Empire gained power in northern Africa. The Aksum Empire traded goods with Arabia, India, and Rome. The Aksum Empire lasted for about 800 years.

After the Aksum Empire, Ethiopia's different ethnic groups were not united. The country's boundaries changed often.

Fact!

In 1974, people found a skeleton in the Great Rift Valley. They named her Lucy. Her bones were more than 3 million years old. In some ways she looked like people do today.

Emperor Haile Selassie attends a celebration in Addis Ababa. He ruled Ethiopia from 1930 to 1974.

Emperors ruled Ethiopia until 1974. Haile Selassie was the last Ethiopian emperor. In 1974, soldiers took over the government. After a civil war, Ethiopia formed a democratic government in 1994.

What type of government does Ethiopia have?

Ethiopia is a **federal republic**. The country is divided into nine states. Every five years, the people choose representatives for their state. Everyone who is 18 or older may vote.

The **parliament** is made up of two groups. The House of People's Representatives has 548 members. This group makes laws. It also chooses a president and a **prime minister**. The president is the chief of state. The prime minister is the head of the government.

Fact!

Addis Ababa is the third highest capital city in the world. It is 7,874 feet (2,400 meters) above sea level.

Members of Ethiopia's government meet at the House of Parliament in the capital city, Addis Ababa.

The House of Federation is the other part of parliament. It has 108 members. They represent the nine state governments. Each state chooses representatives to the House of Federation.

What kind of housing does Ethiopia have?

Most Ethiopians live in rural areas. Their houses are usually round. The wooden frames are covered with straw and clay. Grass or straw is used for the roof.

In large cities, many people live in modern houses and apartments. Other Ethiopians live in mud houses similar to rural ones.

Where do people in Ethiopia live?

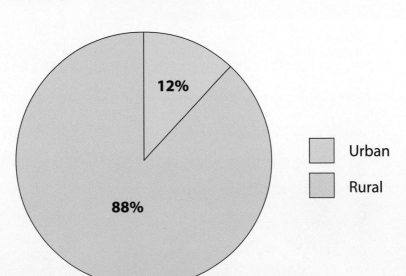

12%

88%

Urban

Rural

Two-story round huts are common in the Lalibela area.

In the desert, some Ethiopians move from place to place to find water and grass. These **nomads** raise cattle, goats, and camels. They build their huts with stick frames and straw mats. The huts are easy to take down when they move.

What are Ethiopia's forms of transportation?

Ethiopian cities have modern forms of transportation. Cars, buses, minibuses, and taxis crowd the streets. A train system connects Addis Ababa to the Gulf of Aden. Large cities have airports.

Mountain villages are hard to reach by car or bus. Many Ethiopians must use donkeys and horses to transport goods and people.

Lake Tana is the largest lake in Ethiopia. Fishers use boats made from reeds that grow in the lake.

Crowds of people make their way through traffic in Addis Ababa.

In rural areas, most roads are dirt.
Most Ethiopians in rural areas must walk.
Some people ride donkeys or mules. In
the desert, people ride camels.

What are Ethiopia's major industries?

Most Ethiopians grow crops and raise animals. Coffee is the most important **export** crop. Ethiopians grow coffee, but it also grows wild in the western highlands. Many people work in the coffee industry. They grow, pick, or process coffee beans.

What does Ethiopia import and export?	
Imports	*Exports*
animals	coffee
food	gold
textiles	leather
vehicles	oilseeds

Some Ethiopians work in the coffee industry sorting coffee beans.

Farmers grow wheat and grains. Teff is an Ethiopian grain that is used to make bread. Teff straw is used to feed animals.

During some years, Ethiopia does not have enough rain. Many farmers lose their crops during these dry times.

What is school like in Ethiopia?

Government schools are free for all children from grade school through high school. In the past, children did not have to go to school. Today, the government requires children to attend school for six years. More students go to school now than in the past.

In large cities, classes are very crowded. Ethiopia does not have enough schools or teachers.

Fact!

Before 1970, only 4 percent of Ethiopians could read and write. Today, more than 42 percent can read and write.

Children in a crowded math class must share desks.

Many Ethiopian children do not go to school. Children of nomads move often and live far from schools. Farm children must take care of their animals.

What are Ethiopia's favorite sports and games?

Soccer is the most popular sport in Ethiopia. There are many professional and local teams. Thousands of people watch national games at the Addis Ababa Stadium. The African Cup of Nations is sometimes held there. International soccer matches are shown on Ethiopian TV.

Fact!

Kenenisa Bekele won an Olympic gold medal in 2004 for the 10,000-meter (6-mile) run.

Ethiopian runners compete during the Athens 2004 Summer Olympic Games.

Ethiopia has many good distance runners. The country's runners often win gold medals in long races. In 1992, Derartu Tulu was the first Ethiopian woman to win an Olympic gold medal. She won the gold again in 2000 for the 10,000-meter (6-mile) race.

What are the traditional art forms in Ethiopia?

Ethiopia is known for its Christian art. Churches have colorful wall paintings that show scenes from the Bible. Women **embroider** cloth for church members and leaders.

Arts and crafts are popular in Ethiopia. People in different areas make pottery and baskets in bright colors to sell.

Fact!

In Lalibela, ancient Christians carved 11 churches out of a mountain. The churches are 800 years old. The roofs of the churches are even with the ground.

Women weave patterned baskets in the city of Harrar.

Music and dancing are part of every celebration. Traveling musicians and singers go from town to town. Sometimes, the singers make up new stories as they sing.

What major holidays do Ethiopians celebrate?

Most holidays in Ethiopia are Christian or Muslim. Ethiopian Christians celebrate Christmas about two weeks after the United States and Canada. The most important Christian holiday is *Timkat*. This holiday celebrates the **baptism** of Jesus Christ. Children often get presents on that day.

What other holidays do people in Ethiopia celebrate?

Labor Day
Maskal
National Day
New Year's Day

Ethiopians celebrate Timkat *with a parade in Lalibela.*

Ethiopian Muslims celebrate the holy month of Ramadan. During Ramadan, most Muslims do not eat or drink during the day. At the end of Ramadan, Muslims celebrate Eid al-Fitr. Families get together and cook special foods.

What are the traditional foods of Ethiopia?

Ethiopians have bread at every meal. The bread is called *injera*. It looks like a thick pancake. Women serve the bread on a low table. They put stew or vegetables on the bread. Chicken stew is very popular.

Families sit around the low table. Each person breaks off a piece of bread. They scoop the stews with the bread.

Cooked beef and vegetables are often put on top of Ethiopian bread.

An Ethiopian woman prepares traditional pancake-like bread.

Coffee is a popular drink in Ethiopia. Coffee is served after meals. One **legend** says that coffee came from western Ethiopia. The area where coffee still grows wild is called Kaffa.

What is family life like in Ethiopia?

Ethiopia has more than 70 different ethnic groups. Each group speaks a different language. Every group also has its own special customs.

Ethiopia's civil war changed family life. Many men died in the war. Now, women must work alone to feed their children.

What are the ethnic backgrounds of people in Ethiopia?

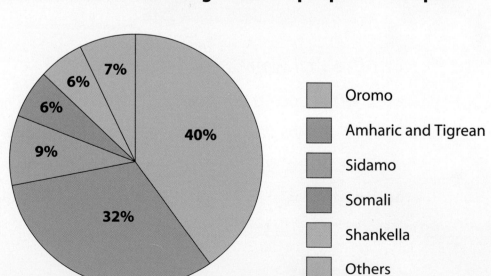

- Oromo
- Amharic and Tigrean
- Sidamo
- Somali
- Shankella
- Others

An Ethiopian nomad family gathers outside their hut in the Great Rift Valley.

In the 1980s and 1990s, Ethiopia had many times when there was not enough rain. Many people died because there was not enough food and water. Others moved to cities or special camps to find food. Some never returned to their villages.

Ethiopia Fast Facts

Official name:

Federal Democratic Republic of Ethiopia

Land area:

432,312 square miles (1,119,683 square kilometers)

Average annual precipitation (Addis Ababa):

49 inches (124 centimeters)

Average January temperature (Addis Ababa):

61 degrees Fahrenheit (16 degrees Celsius)

Average July temperature (Addis Ababa):

60 degrees Fahrenheit (15.5 degrees Celsius)

Population:

67,851,281 people

Capital city:

Addis Ababa

Languages:

Amharic, Tigrinya, Oromigna, and more than 75 others

Natural resources:

copper, gold, hydropower, natural gas, platinum

Religions:

Muslim	*45%*
Ethiopian Orthodox Christian	*35%*
Animist	*12%*
Others	*8%*

Money and Flag

Money:

Ethiopia's money is the birr. One birr equals 100 Ethiopian cents. In 2005, one U. S. dollar equaled 8.68 birr. One Canadian dollar equaled 7.12 birr.

Flag:

The Ethiopian flag is green, yellow, and red. Green stands for labor, yellow for hope, and red for freedom and equality. In 1996, the government added a yellow star in the center stripe. The blue circle represents peace. The star represents a bright future for all Ethiopians.

Learn to Speak Amharic

Most people in Ethiopia speak Amharic. It is Ethiopia's official language. Learn to speak some Amharic words using the chart below.

English	Amharic	Pronunciation
hello	halo	(HA-lo)
good-bye	dehna hunu	(DE-he-na hoo-NOO)
please	ibakkwon	(ee-BAHK-won)
thank you	ammessegnalehu	(AM-me-se-nah-LE-hoo)
yes	aw	(AW)
no	aye	(EYE)
How are you?	indemin allachihu	(een-DE-meen ah-la-CHEE-choo)
I'm fine	tiru	(TEE-roo)

Glossary

baptism (BAP-ti-zuhm) —the Christian tradition of putting water on people's heads to accept them into the religion

embroider (em-BROI-dur)—to sew a design onto cloth

emperor (EM-pur-ur)—the ruler of an empire

export (EK–sport)—a good sent to another country for sale there

federal republic (FED-uh-ruhl ri-PUHB-lik)—a government of states led by a president or prime minister with officials elected by voters

highland (HYE-luhnd)—a mountainous region of a country

legend (LEJ-und)—a story handed down from earlier times

nomad (NOH-mad)—a person who moves from place to place to find food and water

parliament (PAR-luh-muhnt)—the group of people who have been elected to make laws in some countries

prime minister (PRIME MIN-uh-stur)—the leader of a parliament, a government body that makes laws

Internet Sites

FactHound offers a safe, fun way to find Internet sites related to this book. All of the sites on FactHound have been researched by our staff.

Here's how:
1. Visit *www.facthound.com*
2. Type in this special code **073684354X** for age-appropriate sites. Or enter a search word related to this book for a more general search.
3. Click on the **Fetch It** button.

FactHound will fetch the best sites for you!

Read More

Delzio, Suzanne. *Ethiopia.* Many Cultures, One World. Mankato, Minn.: Blue Earth Books, 2003.

Heinrichs, Ann. *Ethiopia.* Enchantment of the World. New York: Children's Press, 2005.

Macknish, Neil and Elizabeth Berg. *Welcome to Ethiopia.* Welcome to My Country. Milwaukee: Gareth Stevens Publishing, 2001.

Morris, Noelle. *Ethiopia.* Steadwell Books World Tour. Chicago: Raintree, 2004.

Index